Deborah C. Aalbers
Illustrated by Daniel Wlodarski

Moos, Mud, Mayhem!

Title: Moos, Mud, Mayhem!
Illustrator: Daniel Wlodarski

Electronic book ISBN 978-1-7388446-0-9
Softcover ISBN 978-1-7388446-2-3
Hardcover ISBN 978-1-7388446-1-6

I hope this story will give you loads of giggles. Happy reading!
Deborah.

For my Grandsons,
whose laughter I cherish
and
For my Dad,
who always believed I would write children's books

***

Special Thanks
The author would like to thank the cows
in the pasture behind her house
for their help with this story.

Ellie stood at the fence by the
Meeting Tree and kicked a board
with her hoof.
Thump, thump, thump!
She and her friends had gathered
there to plan their day.

"What are we doing today?" asked Luna.

?
THUMP
THUMP
THUMP

"Eat grass," said Nora.

"Laze in the barn," said Grace.

"Walk in a circle?" said Claire.

"I'm so bored," moaned Ellie.
"I'm tired of this pasture."

Thump, thump...
Thump, CRACK!

Ellie's eyes flew open wide.
There was a hole in the fence!
"Hey, I have an idea!" said Ellie.
"Let's go play in the street."

"I don't think we should," whispered Grace. "We'll get into trouble."

"Oh, come on, scaredy-cow," laughed Ellie. "What could happen?"

All the cows tried to push through the hole at the same time.

"Moooooove!" they shouted.

"Me first!" said Ellie.

On the other side of the fence, the cows munched on the soft, fragrant grass of the lawns. It felt silkier on their rough tongues than their pasture grass.

"Hey, look!" said Ellie. "There's an open garage door. I have an idea!"

Inside, Ellie found a barbecue, Nora found hockey sticks, Claire found skis, Luna found silly hats.

"I have an idea! Let's have a party!" Ellie sang out.

"But, these things don't belong to us," said Grace.

"Oh, that's OK.
The people won't mind,"
said Ellie.

The cows partied.

They frolicked.

They twirled and leaped.

Soon, mud squished and
squelched under their hooves.

THUD!

Grace lost her balance and landed rump-first in the gooey mud.

"Help!" she cried. "I'm stuck!"

"Don't worry," said Ellie. "I have an idea."

Ellie arranged the cows around Grace.
The cows behind Grace pushed.
The cows in front pulled.

"Moooooove!" groaned the cows.
But Grace did not budge.

Ellie furrowed her fuzzy brow and thought.
Then a smile danced across her face.

"Don't worry," she said. "I have an idea.
Nora, get the hockey sticks.
Claire, bring the skis."

Ellie arranged the cows again.
The cows behind Grace pushed.
The cows in front pulled.
"Moooooove!" they groaned.
But Grace did not budge.

Warm tears streamed down Grace's long face. "I'm stuck in this cold, slimy mud, and now my tummy hurts, too," she wailed.

"Come on," Ellie said to her friends. "Let's see what we can find to help."

Ellie, Nora, Claire and Luna found a ladder, ropes and pulleys. Ellie furrowed her fuzzy brow and thought.

"Don't worry," she said after a moment. "I have an idea!"

"Claire, tie this rope around Grace's belly. Luna, hold the ladder against that tree."

Ellie climbed up, attached a pulley to the tree's sturdy branches, then ran the other end of the rope through it.

"NOW!" she called.

The cows behind Grace pushed.
The cows in front pulled.

"Moooooove!"

Everyone heaved.
Ever so slowly,
Grace began to unstick from the gooey mud.

Suddenly.....

All the cows let out one GIANT, ENORMOUS, HUMONGOUS FART!

Grace shot out of the mud, sailed high into the air and came down with a THWUMP! on the mucky pavement.

"I don't think the barbecued grass was such a good idea," moaned Claire.

"Cars!" yelled Nora. "The people are coming home!"

"Oh no!" cried Ellie. "We're in big trouble!

RUUUUUUUUUN!"

Slippery mud squished and sucked at the cows' hooves, but couldn't stop them as they dashed for the hole in the fence.

The cows in the front pushed. The cows in the back pushed some more.

"Moooooooooove!" shouted the cows.

"Quick! Everyone hide!" whispered Ellie.

The cows huddled together behind some large bushes and waited.

The people grumbled as they cleaned up the cows' muddy mess. Then they patched the fence and went to bed.

When the people were gone, the cows tip-toed out from their hiding places and gathered under the Meeting Tree.

"Well, hmmph!" Ellie sighed. "I guess it's no more adventures for us!"

"Oh, don't be too sure," said Grace, her eyes twinkling. "You never know what fun tomorrow might bring!"

Manufactured by Amazon.ca
Bolton, ON